# What Our Readers Have Said...

*"The Pinpoint Training Series delivers information that could be used in a lot different areas."*

•

*"Applicable and valid. The information is good."*

•

*"I like this because I can take them with me to read at a convenient time. I feel the little time I have to spend in the office is best use on activities that directly relate to revenue opportunities. I like the short amount of time it takes to keep up with these."*

•

*"I just read each book, and then file it for future reference."*

•

*"My thought is that the real value of these books comes into effect when doing the action plans."*

•

*"The challenge when I think a specific topic does not apply is to find a way to make it apply."*

•

*"Easy to use, understand, and reference if needed."*

•

*"Good layout and to the point."*

•

*"I think a lot of the recommendations in these books are very useful, and can be applicable to everyday situations. If nothing else, it's a good reference guide to fall back upon if a situation arises in the future."*

•

*"These books are relevant to today's work environment and the ongoing change in the way we manage our workforce."*

•

*"These books will pay for the time that I am investing. There are numerous good ideas that will streamline what I do and how I do it."*

•

*"All and all I think the Pinpoint series is a good program. I know other people I would love to have something like this. I think a lot of the suggestions are very useful, and can be applicable to everyday situations. If nothing else it's a good reference guide to fall back upon if a situation arises in the future."*

•

*"These books reinforce many concepts that I have learned through seminars, schooling and other programs. For myself, it serves as a constant learning tool that keeps me on top of the issues that many of us encounter every day."*

•

*"All in all, I think you have good training books. It helps everyone to review these materials, it serves as a good reminder to us on how to conduct ourselves."*

•

*"The information is valuable in these books."*

•

*"Good thoughts and ideas."*

•

*"I believe these books would be valuable to all employees."*

•

# Financial Analysis & Budgeting

*Pinpoint Management Skill Development Training Series*

TIMOTHY F. BEDNARZ

MAJORIUM
BUSINESS PRESS

Pinpoint Management Skill Development Training Series
*"Financial Analysis & Budgeting"*
Timothy F. Bednarz

Graphic design: Monika Pawlak

Majorium Business Press
2025 Main Street
Stevens Point, WI 54481
715.342.1018 • 800.654.4935



ISBN 978-1-882181-71-1

Printed in the United States of America

# Introduction

*The Pinpoint Management Skill Development Training Series* is designed for targeted training and education regarding increased improvement in a specific skill or competency.

Each book within this series is designed to be easy to use, understand and apply to your job. It can be used as a basis for training individuals, as a discussion guide or as a personal training tool.

Each chapter within this book discusses a specific concept. When you have completed all eight chapters you should have a 360° perspective of the topic.

Additionally, each chapter is divided into specific sections:

- The first section provides you with an overview of the topic
- The Implications section discusses why the concept is important, and why it is important to learn and apply.
- The Strategies, Tips & Techniques to Apply section teaches how to use and apply the particular concept to your work.
- The Points to Ponder section gives you something to think about or to be discussed with a group setting. These are questions not meant to be immediately answered, but to be pondered over time.
- The Training Activity section provides you with the tools to transfer what you have learned to your job. It is designed to help create an action plan to effectively apply the concept.

Each of the topics in this series is time-tested and proven in the marketplace. They have been used by thousands of employees as training tools. Many of the users have commented that what made these books valuable, was the ability to refer to them when a problem surfaced. They indicated that they remembered reading about the exact problem. They referred back to these books and found an appropriate solution.

You will find them equally valuable as a resource in your professional development library.

# Table of Contents

## LEARNING OBJECTIVES:

- To identify and apply the essential elements of effective financial analysis.
- The role of assumptions in analysis and budgeting.
- To apply the effective use of financial analysis tools.
- To interpret the application of financial analysis tools.

# 1

# The Concept and Role of Financial Analysis

Preparing a budget using the principles and practice of financial analysis requires a strategic assessment of various factors, including, but not exclusive to monetary revenues and expenditures. The process is based upon: establishing a set of goals and objectives to guide decision making, assessing departmental needs, priorities, challenges and opportunities, providing an administrative plan of who does what, creating a budget calendar to specify when each task is to be done, accurately estimating revenue expected during the coming year, and accurately estimating the outflow of capital during the coming year.

## IMPLICATIONS — WHAT THIS MEANS TO YOU

In order to hit projections and effectively balance the budget as planned, the first step is to establish goals and objectives for the coming year. Within each department, goals must be tailored to fit specific initiatives, which can be clearly conveyed to the staff and budget officer, supervisor or the personnel put in charge of budget oversight.

Some of the questions that could be addressed include: Does the department need a new computer system? or, Does the department need to make major improvements to its existing infrastructure? or, Where does the department need to strengthen its programs and/or services? as well as, Does the department need to incorporate new employees? and, What within the department needs immediate attention, and what things can wait?

## STRATEGIES, TIPS & TECHNIQUES TO APPLY

Specific actions need to be taken in an organized fashion to generate a proper, realistic budget. The steps are as follows:

### Assessing Departmental Needs

It is extremely important to assess and regularly reexamine needs and priorities in order to adjust and adapt to changing conditions. In addition, planning and evaluating budgeting procedures, personnel needs and priorities need to be addressed. As part of the financial analysis budgeting process it is necessary to accurately estimate revenue and expenditures to provide information about meeting the costs of all programs and services.

### Complete an Administrative Plan

The administrative plan describes the various steps involved in the budget process and the persons to whom these responsibilities are assigned. It is a statement of policy that documents the actions that must be completed in the course of the budget preparation process and the sequence of these actions. It also designates the individual(s) responsible for each action. A sound administrative plan is essential to ensure orderliness and accountability within the budget process.

### Components of an Administrative Plan

It is important to take necessary steps to ensure accuracy and budgetary expediency for approval. As part of the process, under each budget heading, one needs to define who will be responsible for the detailed steps that need to be taken. Accompanying this, notes should be attached that define what is expected, when it is expected and how things need to be done.

This step-by-step planning process begins with:

- Initiating the budget preparation process
- Preparing a budget calendar, listing all steps to be taken and target dates for the budget preparation process
- Sending the budget memo to all department heads
- Preparing and distributing budget request forms and information packets to all departments
- Meeting with the department heads and assisting them with completion of their budget requests
- Department heads complete and return budget request forms to the budget officer or other designated personnel
- Preparing revenue estimates
- Completing the proposed budget
- Sending the proposed budget on for approval with the following support information for each fund, which includes a:
    - Budget message
    - Budget summary
    - Summary of revenue sources
    - Summary of department expenditures
- The organizational director or whoever is in charge of overseeing all budgets then reviews the proposed budget and makes any necessary changes and redistributes it.
- The budget should then be entered into the organizational accounting system.
    - Copies of the budget can be distributed to department heads, and other interested parties who request it. In the case of a large budget document, it might be useful to include copies of the detailed summary.

## The Budget Calendar

The budget calendar establishes procedural deadlines. In some cases, the budget officer receives all of the budget requests from the department heads, and submits them essentially unchanged to whoever is in charge over the total budgeting process for action.

In other cases, the budget officer assembles all the departments' budget requests and uses them to prepare a preliminary budget. This proposed budget would be given to the designated organizational budget director for review and revision. Regardless of the person designated to serve as the budget officer, a clearly defined framework should be established to ensure that all department heads know who is responsible for each function. Also, it is a good idea to adopt a written policy for the budget officer that clearly outlines each specific departmental goal and objective for the coming year.

The budget calendar lists the steps and suggested timelines for completion of the various phases of budget development. The main purpose of the calendar is to alert department heads, officials and other necessary staff to the expected completion of each stage of the budget process. Within the calendar, it is important to develop three separate groupings: "Required Date," "Action Steps Needed," and the "Responsible Party or Parties."

The length of time required to complete each procedure in the budget process will depend on several factors, such as the complexity of the organizational structure, the experience and expertise of the staff, the intensity of the debate over the proposed budget, and the time consumed in reviewing and adopting it. In smaller companies, three months is sufficient to complete the budget cycle; a medium-sized organization may need four months or more.

## Generating Departmental Requests

It is essential for the department heads to be involved in the budget process. Department heads are the best source of information on departmental financial history, and are most qualified to identify both needs and opportunities for budget cutbacks. Utilizing the knowledge and abilities of department heads within the budgeting process is a useful way to advise the organizational governing body about individual departmental accomplishments, proposals of workable alternatives for improving the quality of work, and increased production and services, while highlighting special problems that are facing their various departments.

## Utilizing a Budget Information Packet

Approximately three months prior to the last day of the current fiscal year (earlier for large companies), the budget officer or designated personnel should furnish each department head an information packet. This packet is used to prepare the particular department's budget requests and should include the following:

- A statement of the current budget policy
- Cost factor guidelines such as pay increase levels and other factors appropriate for the budget period
- Price lists, vendors and websites used for the purchase of supplies, equipment, training etc.
- A set of departmental budget request forms, along with detailed instructions for completing the forms and the budget estimates
- Revenue and expenditure guidelines to follow when preparing the budget request forms

## Generating a Budget Policy Statement

The budget officer or designated personnel should draft a budget policy statement. Often this policy statement outlines all organizational as well as departmental goals, objectives and priorities for the coming year.

The budget policy statement should include:

1. The financial outlook for the organization's next fiscal year and a description of major factors that contribute to that outlook.
2. Specific recommendations on the overall budget policy.
3. An itemization of known budget priorities for the next fiscal year.
4. A description of the guidelines the organization expects all department heads to follow in preparing their budget requests for the next fiscal year.

The budget policy statement should be distributed to all department heads and others who will participate in the preparation of the budget for the next fiscal year. Remember, it is important to involve as many staff members as possible in the budget process, particularly the supervisors and the operators of machinery or equipment. These are the individuals who are most familiar with needed equipment repairs, replacements and upgrades. Work with the individuals who have knowledge of certain working conditions and employee expectations since they can provide invaluable planning insights.

## POINTS TO PONDER — SOMETHING TO THINK ABOUT

1. When sending along a proposed budget for approval, do you currently include support information for each fund? Why or why not?
2. Do you personally feel it is necessary to develop a budget policy statement? Other than what was discussed here, what else do you feel it should include?

## TRAINING ACTIVITY — APPLICATION & ACTION PLAN

To save time and to arrive at a consensus it may be advantageous to hold a meeting of all departmental heads. Designating a specific meeting for this purpose will provide a good time and place to hand out budget information packets while conducting a page-by-page review of the material and having an open discussion on issues that are raised in regard to it. The packet should include instructions directing department heads how to compile and submit estimates of their budget needs for the next fiscal year to the designated budget officer.

As part of the process it may be wise to tell the department heads that all estimates should be returned to the designated budget officer at least 60 days before the close of the current fiscal year, and should be set forth in standardized forms such as the ones below.

## Departmental Workload Form

The departmental workload form summarizes the departments' accomplishments during the current year. It explains proposed changes or improvements for the next fiscal year and provides workload statistics, such as costs per employee per year, increased production capacity each year, number of initiatives implemented or expanded upon, etc.

## Departmental Budget Request Form

The departmental budget request form shows the amount actually spent by the departments during the prior fiscal year, the amount budgeted for the current fiscal year, the projected expenditures for the current fiscal year, and the amount the department heads propose to spend during the next fiscal year.

## Departmental Personnel Request Form

This form is used to describe salary and related costs of personnel presently employed and proposed to be employed by the various departments. For smaller companies, the name and job title of individual employees should be listed. For larger companies, the data can be presented for classes or groups of employees.

## Departmental Change-in-Service Form

The departmental change-in-service form shows proposed service changes, the cost of these changes and the number and type of additional personnel required to perform the service.

## Departmental Capital Equipment Outlay Form

The departmental capital equipment outlay form is used to list the acquisition of, or addition to, fixed assets of significant value, such as equipment and departmental infrastructure improvements.

These examples are meant as a basic guideline. Additional forms can be added to generate other information that is needed. Department heads should be encouraged to request all proposed budget needs for manpower, materials and equipment.

- It is important to remember that cutbacks may have to be made in budget requests.
- Input from department heads is essential since some important needs might never come to light unless they are given an opportunity to fully explain their positions.
- This approach offers the advantage of generating more options and alternatives from which the organizational governing body may select.

# 2

# Critical Factors of Success

Operating budgets can be defined as a realistic account or statement of income and cost objectives for an upcoming year. In their essence, operating budgets are plans against which results of actual performance are accurately compared so as to achieve control by detecting and correcting off-standard performance.

The term "budget," when it is used in its broader sense is considered to be a plan that can be used for oversight and control. It can be effectively applied to numerous areas, including inventory and cash flow. An operating budget typically covers a one-year period, and consists of all of the major operating facets and phases of the functions for which the organization and its associated departments exist.

For example, a manufacturing company is in the business of selling one product or several products. Since this is its focus, its operating budget for the year needs to include sales, operational costs, research and development costs, and by deduction, profit. A service company is also in the same vein, selling one or more services. Its operating budget will include and reflect revenue and operating costs, and by deduction, profit.

## IMPLICATIONS – WHAT THIS MEANS TO YOU

Since most operating budgets tend to become statements of objectives, they can also be considered forecasts or estimates. As an effective manager, it becomes part of their responsibility to help establish realistic budgets, while attempting to make sensible, practical and responsible income and cost improvements throughout the budgeted year.

Effective budgets are just one of the devices or means used to help plan for specific performance goals, and for measuring how well they are being attained. Wise managers who budget effectively tend to work to achieve continuous improvements in operational performance. Effective operational budgeting presumes that managers who function within budgets will attempt to do better than what budgetary standards expect of them. They will work to improve and generate more, while spending less. Ineffective budgeters often tend to overspend their allowance allotments, and are more likely to exert pressure for continuous monetary increases.

## STRATEGIES, TIPS & TECHNIQUES TO APPLY

It is important to remember that budgeting does have its limitations. The process should be accepted as only the beginning of adequate control measures, especially in areas of larger costs, particularly in direct labor and raw material ones. Within these two categories most companies need additional cost control measures, which tend to fall beyond what is typically available through their operating budgets alone.

There are several critical factors of budgeting that lead to direct challenges associated with the concept, especially within various types of industries including service-related ones. The factors that tend to surface most frequently are:

### Variances in Budgeting Philosophy

Today as a departmental head or manager, supervisor or foreman, one can expect to work within three categories of companies in regard to their perspectives on budgets and controls. The first is managing within a company that adheres to no budgeting philosophy or application. These companies tend to be smaller in size or at the lower end of the medium-sized company grouping. Many of these may tend to be quite profitable and successful, but no matter how much so, they still can be helped enormously through cost improvements and careful budgeting. This is because without set budgets, no standards can be established in various areas of cost within their organizations, and cost standards are an absolute requirement for cost control. Standards are used as an evaluation measurement tool in order to compare variances and to make accurate calculations.

The second is a company that adheres to a solid philosophy that insists on a well-maintained, effective budget. Organizations that adhere to this philosophy tend to have continual top management buy-in to the importance of budgeting. They award the process enormous amounts of support and attention. These companies tend to become more successful, year after year. However, from numerous research studies, companies within this grouping tend to be in the minority, especially when compared to the third type of organizational philosophy.

The third is a company that operates with an ineffective budget. Most research concludes that the majority of companies tend to fall within this category. Their company budgets are not as dynamic or effective a tool as they could and should be. Most times their budgets need to be revitalized because of numerous weaknesses that exist within the process itself.

## Various Budgeting Weaknesses

It is important watch out for the factors outlined below that deal with major budgeting weaknesses. These work to generate inefficient and ineffective budgets as well as an inability to properly manage and monitor them.

### *Department heads, supervisors and managers ignoring their budgets*

This is usually the result of not being held accountable for budget control and its proper management.

Most times these individuals fail to be called in by their superiors for a review of budget performance, whether it is good or inferior. Typically, two reasons for this exist. Budgets may be considered unrealistic where over a period of time foremen, supervisors, department heads or managers fail to justify their use and applicability. These same people often feel that the budget "cost standard" is extremely poor, being either too high or too low, where they are totally unusable and unreliable.

### *Lack of collaboration among management levels in budget development*

When budgets are devised and are simply made to flow from the very top downward to all the organizational departments, problems and challenges are certain to occur. Department heads, managers and supervisors have no say about what goes into the budgeting process and its development, or the goals being set within them. As they are isolated from important input, their sense of value, expertise and experience diminishes. This in turn oftentimes leads to feelings of "budget resentment," which is hard to overcome.

Until the budget is set in stone and passed on to them, department heads, managers and supervisors do not have any idea of the constraints that they will be expected to work within. This generates excessive amounts of stress and frustration. Often, since the budget process has no direct input from the individuals closest to understanding the actual needs, activities and capital required to fund necessary projects and initiatives, the budgets that are passed down tend to contain serious errors, both from a psychological and technical standpoint.

Once the budget reaches the intended personnel, these errors, omissions and absurdities fail to get communicated back to top management who initially established it. Instead of directly addressing and coming to a consensus on the major issues involved, it often simply becomes normal operating procedure to have accounting allow for variances such as product-costing needs, profit-planning, etc. In any case, companies that rely on implementing budgets only from the top down are left with budgets that are weak and not nearly as effective as they could, or should be.

### *Large variances remain uncorrected*

Variance is defined as the difference between the budget allowance and the actual expenditure.

A favorable cost variance is known as a black or plus variance, which is generated when the budget allowance exceeds the actual money spent. An unfavorable cost variance, known as red or minus variance, is generated when the actual money spent exceeds the budget allowance. However, these meanings tend to become reversed when applied to income or activity. For example, if a budgeted activity is for say, 90,000 units and actual activity is for 100,000 units, there is a favorable 10,000-unit activity variance. If actual activity is only 80,000 units, there exists a 10,000-unit unfavorable variance.

If this weakness exists, it is likely that when a series of budgetary reports are issued, there will be numerous large variances, both favorable as well as unfavorable, showing up month after month. When this occurs, it is an obvious sign that improper or poor budgeting has occurred. This in turn indicates that one or more of the following conditions exist, which should be addressed and corrected:

- Unrealistic or inferior budget standards;
- Extremely inadequate budget maintenance;
- Inadequate or poor management follow up on performance in regard to budget;
- Inappropriate or inferior management policy, such as, "The budget shall remain as initially established for the entire budget year."

***Budget decision makers <u>not</u> getting out into the workplace to observe actual operations***

Often this is viewed as a rather unlikely or inappropriate sign of budgetary weakness, yet it is extremely indicative of budget-related problems. It is impossible to set budgets from behind a desk. When personnel involved in the budgeting effort either fail to take the time or do not have the time or interest to get out to view everyday operations, weak budgets and/or an inadequacy in monitoring them will be experienced.

Most often the causes for this inaction is due to understaffing or what is known as "motivational inertia." Operational budgeting consists of dealing with matters of operation, which are dynamic in nature. The only way to keep current with them is to get out into the various areas of operation as much as possible.

If the individuals responsible for budgeting do not see for themselves what is going on at any point in time, illogical, irrational and ridiculous input and inserts will begin to creep into the budgets.

### *Department heads, supervisors or foremen* *not told how allowances are determined*

When department heads, foremen, and departmental managers do not know or understand how allowances on their budgets are determined, or what kinds of expenses are charged to individual budgeted cost items, it can be expected that the budgets themselves will not become the vital management tool they are intended to be. This is mostly due to the fact that these individuals are not able to understand the data they are supposed to be using, which results in:

- Inadequate initial budgetary training;
- The failure to enforce the training with follow ups and reinforcement programs;
- Too little contact taking place among the budgeting function and operating individuals;
- The lack of management support or insights as to the appropriate use of the budget;
- The failure of collaboration among various department heads and other appropriate individuals within the budgeting process.

### *Lack of improvement action because of the set budget*

Numerous constructive activities may be going on inside a company such as new techniques being employed in any number of operating areas or new planning or fresh control procedures being initiated. Yet, the key question from a budgeting standpoint needs to be, "Which ones were initiated because of what the budgeting process disclosed or revealed?"

Budgets result in generating timely periodic reports. The true test of any report is what specifically results because of it. If either the budget-development steps or the performance-to-budget reports fail to generate or cause any significant changes, it can be assumed that either there is a perfect organization: one that is operating as efficiently and as effectively as it is possibly able (which is extremely unlikely) … or the budgets are not resulting in obtaining needed but necessary improvement action.

Solutions for this can be varied. It usually depends upon top management's vivacity and strength in its belief and use of budgets. The real question all budgeting personnel should ask if no impetus for action comes out of the reporting process is, " What is everyone getting out of the time, effort and expense of this activity?"

***Lack of continuous measurement of budget results***

It is a key fact that good budgeting costs money. The larger and more complex the organization, the greater the cost attached to the process. Budgets demand an investment not only in their designing, installing and implementing aspects, but also a continuing investment in their maintenance and oversight. Well-managed budget measurements can be compared to analyzing a company investment as to an expensive piece of machinery for its production department.

It becomes important to do a post audit, to check to see if the results are what were initially expected and if the capabilities and outputs promised are actually being realized. This same logic needs to apply to the investment of budgeting. If this is not done, it is more likely than not that "too low" or "no return" on budgeting investments and efforts will be obtained rather than positive gains.

There is one truth that never alters in regard to budgeting efforts: When a person can measure something he or she is speaking about, and is able to express it numerically, vast knowledge is gained in regard to it. But, when something cannot be measured or when it cannot be effectively expressed numerically, far less knowledge is acquired.

## POINTS TO PONDER — SOMETHING TO THINK ABOUT

1. Do you feel that budget applications require experienced judgment in more important areas like operations? Why or why not?
2. Do you personally feel it is important and necessary to measure budget results on an ongoing basis? Why or why not?

## TRAINING ACTIVITY — APPLICATION & ACTION PLAN

It is important to recognize that budgets can be helpful rather than disturbing or frustrating. Management needs budgets. In order to help others understand this, take the following action steps as a group:

1. Discuss how budgets tend to generate morale problems and why.
2. Discuss why budgets are often viewed as constraint mechanisms. Address this from both a negative and positive standpoint.
3. Discuss how budgets can be used "against" as well as "for" someone and the factors that work to determine this.
4. Discuss how budgets are an important aspect of the company's overall plan.
5. Address budgeting from a, "What's in it for me?" perspective.
6. Examine what attitudes can destroy effective budget monitoring and reporting.
7. Detail steps everyone can take to help keep certain aspects of the budget within its allotment.
8. Create a list of possible consequences in regard to ineffective budgeting controls, maintenance and monitoring.

# 3

# Understanding the Impact of Financial Analysis

Financial analysis has a definite impact on the budgeting process and includes helping department heads, managers and foremen see why the process is valuable as well as essential. Through the process of solid financial analysis, the answer to the question, "Why budget?" can be addressed in a more detailed and concise manner.

The budgeting process helps to fulfill one's sense of curiosity about organizational as well as departmental priorities and expectations. It also works to: gain and maintain control over operational processes, enhance productivity, gain knowledge about the organization, align departmental activity with the organization's strategic plan, and reveal the expertise that resides within the organization.

## IMPLICATIONS – WHAT THIS MEANS TO YOU

The budgeting process along with the aid of financial analysis helps to strengthen and incorporate an organization's strategic plan. In other words, the budget process helps to "assist or serve" the strategic plan. As such, the strategic plan causes or creates the budget, not the other way around.

Budgets in their truest sense are considered to be "political," and are created for a specific entity and to cover a definite length of time, which becomes quantitatively expressed. This is one of the main reasons why financial analysis has such a large role to play in the budgeting process, and why it has such an impact on it as well.

## STRATEGIES, TIPS & TECHNIQUES TO APPLY

### Independent Roles Within Budgeting

Department heads, supervisors and foremen have an important role to play regarding budgeting and financial analysis. By gaining more familiarity and expertise within the process of budgeting they are better able to: understand departmental financial needs, collaborate with the budgeting director and become knowledgeable about organizational as well as departmental goals, become more aware of the department's previous financial performance, gain insights and knowledge as to how budget funding is determined, and understand the basics of reporting requirements and procedural steps for justifying funding for particular projects and activities.

### Why Budgeting Efforts Fail to Generate Expected Outcomes

Often budgeting is disliked because its purpose and function is not completely understood. Most individuals see a budget as a hindrance or obstruction to accomplishing things in a creative, flexible manner. Budgeting also tends to be viewed as something that prevents accomplishing one's personal thoughts, beliefs and ideas about departmental goals and objectives. It is also looked upon as limiting one's ability to incorporate certain initiatives, projects and activities that may allow the department to function and operate more smoothly. In addition, many fear budgeting out of concern that it will reveal personal weaknesses and shortcomings.

### The Positive Side of Budgeting

Through solid financial analysis and planning, budgets are designed to impact departmental units in a constructive way and each should become oriented to help the organization accomplish its overall goals and objectives. The budget should help each department adhere to realistic plans of action while providing a framework for evaluating performance and improving budget planning. Each departmental entity should become participatory in helping to monitor and maintain budget control as it works to enhance rather than block opportunities. Finally, in order to generate a substantial positive impact, budgets should: be investigative, generate ideas, be objective, and generate innovation.

## The Impact of Budgetary Data Collection

The budgeting process not only impacts bottom-line finances but can also be expected to enhance and provide:

- Collaborative understanding of human resource policies such as job sharing, benefit costs and training expenditures
- A guide in helping to define better job descriptions
- A clearer understanding of what the department does, why it is important, how it operates, and with whom
- A clearer understanding of current staff capability
- Facility planning insights such as the departmental cost per square foot when fully functional and operational
- Square footage requirements that need to be devoted to project activity, people and equipment

## Gathering More Information About the Organization

A budget forces departmental heads to answer important questions such as:

- What does the organization want from the department?
- What does the organization want to accomplish?
- How is the department interpreting the organization's vision?
- How is the department performing against that vision?

## Budgeting with Financial Analysis Impacts Benchmarking and Measuring

Benchmarking and measuring efforts help to adequately keep budgets on track as well as to identify and define areas that require greater budgetary spending.

The two functions of benchmarking and measuring have a positive impact since each: makes it possible to evaluate resources, activity and costs, fosters innovation, supports viability, reveals core competencies, and defines value.

## To Measure or Not to Measure

One of the purposes of benchmarking and measuring is to ensure that departmental employees see the big picture as to what is going on within the organization at various points of time. The impact of budgeting and measuring for results oftentimes gets pushed aside. There are many reasons for this, but mostly it is due to:

- Suspecting that we won't learn anything that we don't already know
- Being afraid that results will be used against us
- Being afraid that we will be judged by unfair standards
- Being confused as to what system to use
- Believing that benchmarking and measuring is expensive and time-consuming for what it will reveal
- Confusion as to where value lies

## Benchmarking and Measuring Through Balanced Scorecard

The term "Balanced Scorecard" comes from a 1992 Harvard Business Review article, "The Balanced Scorecard – Measures That Drive Performance" by Kaplan and Norton. The approach uses Key Performance Indicators or (KPI's), which are financial and non-financial metrics to quantify objectives to reflect strategic performance of an organization.

Using the Balanced Scorecard concept is an effective way to translate shareholder expectations into key performance indicators for an organization and is a comprehensive method or system that allows for the monitoring of organizational performance to complement financial measures.

## KPIs

KPIs are used to assess the present state of the organization and to prescribe a course of action. The process of monitoring KPI's in real-time is known as "business activity monitoring." They are frequently used to "value" difficult to measure activities, such as the benefits of leadership development and engagement, service and satisfaction. KPI's are typically tied to an organization's strategy and tend to differ depending on the nature of the organization. They help the organization to measure progress toward its goals, especially toward difficult to quantify knowledge-based processes.

A KPI is an important part of a *measurable objective*, which is constructed as follows: direction, KPI, benchmark, target and time frame. In the example, "We want to increase average revenue per customer from $20 to $35 by EOY 2008." The KPI is "average revenue per customer." KPI's should not be confused with a *critical success factor*. In the above example, a critical success factor would be something that needs to be put in place to achieve that objective, such as a product launch.

By measuring and monitoring operational efficiency, employee performance and innovation, customer satisfaction, as well as financial performance, long-term strategies can be linked to short-term actions. Within most companies, traditional measures tend to be financial in nature. While, it is true that no organization can survive if it ignores these measures, few organizations will grow and prosper if they only pay attention to financial matters. The Balanced Scorecard approach takes a wider view to accommodate other areas and factors of measurement.

## POINTS TO PONDER — SOMETHING TO THINK ABOUT

1. By gaining more familiarity with the process of budgeting, how do feel you would be better able to help your department as well as organization?
2. In what ways do you feel that benchmarking and measuring efforts can help to keep budgetary costs on track?

## TRAINING ACTIVITY — APPLICATION & ACTION PLAN

As part of the budgeting process it is important to leave room for innovation and opportunity. To help incorporate some items into the budget for innovation purposes, considering doing the following:

1. Brainstorm for new initiatives.
2. Develop ways to prepare the staff for a state of change.
3. Build change management into the departmental vision.
4. Develop strategies for creating a seed fund for new opportunities.

# 4

# Common Budgeting and Financial Analysis Problems

Budgetary personnel that adopt and apply a dedicated financial analysis approach to planning and budgeting are able to achieve greater accuracy, and will have less budget-related challenges to overcome. They are also able to plan and budget more consistently across their departments and organization.

Budget management is one of the most important aspects of a budgetary leader's job. However, even the best of them often tend to lack a thorough understanding of processes, procedures, and responsibilities that are associated with effective budgeting and financial management. Several factors often tend to contribute to budget-related problems. As part of the budget analysis and the financial evaluation process, it is important to identify just why efforts to follow as well as maintain and control a set budget were ineffective. The process must also include identifying factors that lead to disclosing why the end results of the budget investment fell way short of expectations.

## IMPLICATIONS – WHAT THIS MEANS TO YOU

In numerous cases, it is easy for many departmental heads to recognize that a majority of programs often end up costing far more than expected and take far longer to develop and implement than originally planned. When reviewing past budgeting, one may find that results often are tied to several common problems.

For instance, requirements for what certain specific initiated activities needed to do and associated performance expectations often are not adequately defined at the beginning of a program, or are sometimes significantly changed once a program has already begun. In addition, investment practices are sometimes weak. As such, potentially more cost-effective approaches are not fully examined and cost estimates often become overly optimistic. Often, administrative strategies are poorly executed. This is typically seen with inadequate oversight of projects and their related activities. Finally, technologies are often not incorporated thoroughly enough to be included into ongoing project development and reporting.

When addressing these common budgeting issues it is essential to ask the following four questions:

1. Does the budget appear to be accurate?
2. Does the budgeting process approach include collaboration among various departmental members?
3. Does more time and effort go into analyzing rather than managing budget-related information and data?
4. Does the budget-related planning cycle appear to be as efficient and effective as it should be?

## STRATEGIES, TIPS & TECHNIQUES TO APPLY

If any of the above questions were answered in the negative, it is likely there are challenges that need to be overcome. Four typical budgetary issues or concerns are detailed below, as well as what to do about them.

### Problem One: Collaboration

If individuals rely on incorporating only spreadsheets for budgetary purposes, there is little likelihood that any collaboration is taking place within the budgeting process. Spreadsheet analysis falls short because it is not designed to facilitate collaboration. In order to overcome this challenge, it is essential to make information open and accessible so that everyone can collaborate effortlessly and effectively. To do this, make sure individuals at all levels of the organization have access to the information they need, in real time. One of the best ways to accomplish this is to consider automating the consolidation of data through a centralized database to promote collaboration and efficiency. Unfortunately, relying solely on budget-related spreadsheet applications falls short in allowing budgetary personnel to do this as it does not allow for the current tracking of data.

To track current data it is important to make certain that the database is always up-to-date and is relied upon as the sole source of information. The entire organization can benefit when all departmental managers are allowed to access and update their budget information and have it automatically consolidated into the corporate plan of the organization. The net gain of effective budget information is seen in having the most current data to make informed decisions more rapidly.

## Problem Two: Data Accuracy

The most common issues around budgeting and planning, especially within spreadsheets applications, are broken links and incomplete sums. Broken links and incomplete sums often end up giving users access to too little data rather than too much. Errors can be created in a spreadsheet by simply adding a line or accidentally deleting a formula. Managers and the personnel responsible for overseeing the entire budgetary process easily can become bogged down with the linking of spreadsheets, verifying numbers and updating wrong or out-of-date information.

It is important to be able to provide a sense of structure to your plan's formatting to prevent this from happening. Remember, when too much time is spent on managing data it becomes easier to access and apply formulas and data that are not necessarily relevant. To help prevent other associated challenges it may be more effective to empower certain staff members to help implement a budgeting and planning solution.

It may be a wise move to incorporate a spreadsheet-like interface that will provide structure and security to each plan's data references and formatting. This will give budgetary personnel and other designated users the ability to update the plan without giving them access to formulas and other sensitive data. When doing this, results will no doubt be seen in increased efficiency, improved security, and the assurance that the data is always current and accurate.

A spreadsheet-like interface will also help to take a lot of stress off of managers' shoulders, especially those who are in charge of monitoring and overseeing budget expenditures and the results of their monetary investments. It will aid them much more effectively since they will be more able to work with the data and information instead of having to fix it.

## Problem Three: Cost of Doing Business

Using spreadsheets solely to manage budgeting and forecasting takes a vast amount of effort, which often has a tendency to increase costs. Spreadsheets tend to come preloaded on the computer, so they are viewed as an inexpensive tool. However, managing the process of using and sharing spreadsheets has an attached cost as the time needed to continually update spreadsheet-based data can be quite extensive.

Implementing a solid budgeting and planning approach can cut work hours by up to 50%, which will free up personal resources to work on more valuable tasks. Giving the right people the appropriate tools they need, will effectively allow them to spend more time analyzing information instead of managing and monitoring mountains of data. This can be accomplished by building in process-flow monitoring trigger points as well as security controls.

Applying a solid financial approach to budgeting and planning, together with spreadsheet backup, produces more positive results that are seen in improved efficiency, reduced overhead and cost savings. It is necessary to make certain that time is spent on updating information to reflect the budget's current status, which can be easily done through automating and consolidating data into a centralized database.

Whatever steps are taken it is essential to implement solutions that allow for more data analysis and less data management. Keep in mind that it is not necessary to completely abandon spreadsheet-based budgeting approaches, but it is important to devote a high level of attention to value-added activities.

## Problem Four: Responding Quickly to Change

Gauging the impact of a change in the business or within departments from spreadsheets is difficult and can result in lost opportunities. Business operations today require agility and speed. Decisions are frequently based on the performance "at the moment" in regard to projects, individuals or departments. The ability to know when something is taking a wrong turn before it causes a negative impact is critical.

Implementing a companywide solution makes it easier to review multiple versions of a plan, which quickly improves the response time to market changes. Giving employees the ability to make and see changes in real time reduces the opportunity review and decision cycle. Decisions can be made before market forces and changes cause a negative impact to the business, project or budget resources. The ability to make immediate system changes further helps to eliminate the pain and challenge of adding, modifying or changing departments.

## Thinking Outside the Spreadsheet

Adopting an effective budgeting and planning process means that budget personnel explicitly understand the complexity of the procedure. It is also important to understand the need to improve planning efficiency in order to achieve a closer alignment of objectives, and to gain greater visibility into their financial and operational performance.

Because the range of experience within an organization is going to be broad, it is particularly critical that budgeting and planning applications are easy to use. Users at all levels must be able to enter and manage data effectively in order to achieve the desired results. A good budget planning's interface should look and feel like an actual spreadsheet, but with more flexibility.

In addition, a solid budgeting and planning approach must be adaptable to, or at least synergistic with, other existing current models and approaches. Any and all budgeting approaches should be incorporated with the end user in mind. Make certain that the entire budgeting process is addressed and completed through a solid financial analysis of all data.

## POINTS TO PONDER — SOMETHING TO THINK ABOUT

1. What specific factors other than the ones addressed do you feel tend to contribute to budget-related problems and challenges?
2. Do you feel there are shortcomings attached to spreadsheet analysis for budgeting and planning? If so, what are they?

## TRAINING ACTIVITY — APPLICATION & ACTION PLAN

Planning efforts should allow departments as well as the organization to focus on incorporating the right information and data, not on the technology being used to produce final budgetary numbers and monetary resources.

Keep in mind the shortcomings of spreadsheets. They are necessary, but are not the "be all and end all" of the budgeting process. Together with other departmental staff members, discuss the following issues:

- Why spreadsheets are not an effective collaborative tool, while determining what specific things could be implemented into the budgetary and financial analysis process to accommodate more collaboration.
- Why spreadsheets are not always accurate, while identifying what methods or applications could be employed to improve or enhance them.
- Why spreadsheets are not unto themselves scalable or flexible, while determining what things could be incorporated to make budgetary data and information more scalable and flexible.
- Why spreadsheets are not designed to process complex data efficiently or effectively, while identifying specific things that could be done to overcome this deficiency.
- Why spreadsheet analysis does not offer anyone the means to take advantage of possible opportunities, while identifying things that can be applied to help take advantage of them.

# 5

# Budgeting and Analysis Strategies

Budgeting is a method that is necessary to help oversee and keep track of organizational as well as departmental funds. It is considered to be a tool for planning, overseeing and maintaining control of monetary resources.

A budget is a formal, written guide that describes organizational or departmental goals for the future, which becomes expressed in financial terms that cover a given period of time, typically a year. A properly defined budget becomes a detailed statement of estimated income as well as incurred expenses and capital outlay. In essence, a solid budget becomes a historical record of organizational or departmental activities during this given time frame.

## IMPLICATIONS — WHAT THIS MEANS TO YOU

Proper budgeting allows the refining of specific goals so that they are based on realistic resources. One of the main purposes of budgeting is to make certain that available funds are used wisely and efficiently, in an organized manner. A solid budget provides the means for gaining accurate information that allows for adjusting, effectively analyzing and objectively evaluating various organizational as well as departmental programs and activities. Without effective budgeting it becomes impossible to gain practical historical data and information that can be used as a reference and effectively applied for future planning endeavors.

## STRATEGIES, TIPS & TECHNIQUES TO APPLY

One of the main strengths of budgeting is that it easily transforms into an effective tool for good decision making. To begin the process it is best to review the budget already in place for the existing year before attempting to generate a new one. A good time to do this is about two or more months prior to the close of the current year. This allows enough time without worrying about gaining budget approval for the upcoming year. Once the current budget is thoroughly reviewed and analyzed, it becomes time to use the following procedures to help prepare a new solid budget:

### Prepare an Outline of Planned Activities for the Upcoming Year

An outline helps to determine what plans, priorities and activities are important to pursue during the upcoming year. Many times employees, superiors and other organizational department heads will be able to offer proposals for the priorities and activities for consideration throughout the organization's fiscal year. Once done, these proposals should be presented to the budget committee, which is no doubt a separate group of organizational or departmental members, or in some cases, an executive committee that has been formed to deal with budgetary issues. This step is necessary to complete, since all program initiatives and most related activities require money. In essence, these become the "drivers" of the budget itself.

### Determine Available Funds

Determining available funds requires assessing the carry-over balance from the previous year, and identifying the cash that is on hand, as well as other sources of available income and its total. Once done it becomes time to:

- Do a careful analysis of various funding sources, as well as costs and estimated financial additions, if any may exist.
- Estimate expected income and when it is to become available, as through sales or other means.
- Carefully define needed expenses, and detail what they will be used for, such as marketing, advertising, printing, supplies, etc.

- Obtain price quotations on specific required expenditures. Some of this responsibility can be delegated to specific departmental members.

## Rank the Order of Expenditures by Their Importance

This step requires contemplating specific initiatives and activities that would be the wisest use of available funds. Begin to negotiate with necessary departmental members in order to eliminate less essential expenditures, or to determine exactly where certain expenditures can be limited. Revise, review, coordinate and cross-reference this information and data.

Once done, assemble the numerical data and information into a final budget, making certain that it is flexible enough to anticipate conditions or contingencies or unanticipated events that might have been overlooked during the initial planning process. This will allow the organization to project its revenues and expenditures for the upcoming fiscal year.

Changes in budgets are often made based on senior executives recommendations, and budgeters must always be cognizant of this fact. Assuming the revised budget is approved, it is typically then presented for final adoption.

## Keys to Managing a Budget

Once a budget is approved and adopted, it requires proper management, as it is an essential part of the organization's financial roadmap for the year. Some budgets can be alterable under certain conditions. However, this generally requires a vote by company executives or a change in organizational policy, and in some cases, company directives or bylaws.

To manage a budget effectively it becomes important to:

- Set and maintain a minimum cash balance
- Formulate general policies and procedures that are needed to achieve specific objectives
- Maintain an accurate log of all financial transactions, including all income and expenses
- Maintain an organizational or departmental record book, while checking and balancing the records periodically

- Prepare periodic reports related to the budget and present them to executive staff or essential others so everyone knows how the budget is being monitored and revised and why

## Produce Monthly Operating Statements

An operating statement is used as a reporting mechanism that details all transactions that have occurred since the previous one. At the end of each statement a balance should be reported. The monthly statement should be reconciled with year-to-date activity so that a clear picture of the exact financial position can be effectively established. A thorough review of the statement will provide the income of the organization or department, its expenses and the resulting cash balance.

## Control Costs

It is important to allow only approved expenditures. Make it a point to assess the budget at predetermined points of time during the budgeted period. After the budgeted period has elapsed, it becomes time to determine the outcome of each expense and revenue. Carefully assess and review actual costs in order to establish priorities for the next budget time period. Developing and maintaining an accurate budget and knowing just how much money your organization or department is able to work with will help to eliminate a shortfall of capital and the stress of having to deal with it.

### POINTS TO PONDER — SOMETHING TO THINK ABOUT

1. Why do you think budgeting is important to decision making?
2. What do you feel is the most difficult part of the budgeting process? Why?

## TRAINING ACTIVITY – APPLICATION & ACTION PLAN

1. On the left side of your budget, segment information and data into four general areas: Revenue, Expense, Capital, and Contingency.
2. Divide the budget form into two columns, which are designated: Previous Year and Current Year
3. Under each of the designated four categories list all items that apply, for example under Expenses:

**Personnel Services**

- Salaries
- Hourly wages
- Fringe benefits
- Etc.

**Operating Expenses**

- Telephone charges
- Internet access charges
- Other communications

**Office Supplies**

- Printing
- Postage
- Equipment repair
- Equipment rental

**Program Expenses (separate budgets prepared for each)**

- Training expenses
- Newsletters

**Travel**

- Outstanding debit
- Miscellaneous

**Capital Outlay**

- List by item

**Contingency**

- List by designated item

**Total Expenses:**

______________

**Balance:**

______________

# 6

# Poor Analysis Techniques

Financial analysis has a definite impact on decisions that determine budgeting effects and outcomes. The financial analysis process along with reporting evaluations may indicate if a current budget approach is adequate enough, or if revisiting the process is necessary.

Companies tend to use budgeting for two reasons: profit planning and operational cost controls. The basis for constructing budgets for a particular purpose requires effective decision making using the various applications of financial analysis and data reporting. The financial analysis process comes into play within all budgeting efforts, but is far more complex and necessary when a flexible budgeting approach is decided upon. A budget can be designed so that it is able to serve both profit planning as well as cost control needs.

## IMPLICATIONS – WHAT THIS MEANS TO YOU

Budgets need to serve the purpose for which they are intended. The decision to apply one type of budget over another depends upon the logic behind its use, which requires a critical mind for determining what makes better sense as far as a budget's ability to obtain desired goals.

Budgets are sometimes used solely for profit planning. The budgeting procedure includes: forecasting expected revenue from sales, expected project operating costs, and then, through the process of deduction, planned pretax profit.

If this approach is decided upon, it includes taking sales, their revenue and associated costs in order to break them down into monthly increments. Once the year begins to unfold, year-to-date sales forecasts are then compared to year-to-date actual sales. Year-to-date budgeted costs are compared to year-to-date actual costs, and by deduction year-to-date planned pretax profit is compared to year-to-date actual pretax profit.

Budgeting can also be used strictly for the purpose of cost control. This approach is generally decided upon if the budget is meant solely for maintaining the control of operating costs. It is important to remember that the term "operating cost control" is not often one that is consistently used. Many companies prefer to have the term replaced by something else like "the cost control department."

Cost control budgeting efforts and decisions are management driven as they establish the budget allowances. These are done for each cost account at the "cost center" or department level. By comparing actual costs against budget allowance, management seeks to achieve control over the operating costs.

## STRATEGIES, TIPS & TECHNIQUES TO APPLY

Even though a budget generally tends to serve one type of purpose, its function and ability to generate the results desired is what determines the decision as to whether a fixed or flexible budget approach should be applied. If a company wishes to design a budget that serves both purposes then the following must be considered:

### Flexible Budgeting

If company operations remain so stable that actual monthly activity always tends to equal predictions, the decision to operate within a flexible budget approach may not be the best choice. However, most companies are not consistently stable. Actual activity within most usually varies from what was predicted. As a result, budgeted cost allowances also vary. This is why flexible budgeting is often a better course of action.

A flexible budget is often referred to as a "variable" budget. Flexible budgeting is the only secure means for comparing actual costs against budgeted standards in order to achieve control in a logical and fair manner. Flexible budgeting is also essential to profit planning, since flexible budgeting allows for the logical comparison of budget allowances with actual costs. In other words, the process provides a comparison on a like basis, which requires flexing budget allowances to the level of actual activity.

When inflexible or fixed budgeting is applied, budget cost allowances tend to be adjusted to the specific level required by the actual activity of the operation, which creates reporting inaccuracies and because of it, ineffective budget control. With flexible budgeting, within departmental performance-to-budget reports, measured actual activity of the department is shown. Also each individual cost item, both the actual money spent as well as the budget allowance for the actual activity is indicated.

## The Need for Budgeting Flexibility

Inflexible or fixed budgeting typically tends to generate morale problems within companies. Experience has taught many department heads, supervisors and foremen that budgets end up becoming a weapon that is used against them. Their interpretations may be inaccurate, but the feelings still remain. When such an attitude prevails, it becomes a definite problem for management.

When budgets are implemented with few morale problems it is likely due to upper management making the decision to:

- Thoroughly educate and indoctrinate people within the lower levels as to the company's need for budgets. While it is true that a budget is a constraint mechanism, it is a necessary one because it is a major means for the company to plan and control its overall operations.
- Offer a detailed explanation as to how departmental budgets fit into the entire organizational program and structure.
- Detail how the results affect the whole organizational picture as well as future initiatives and goals.
- Outline how achieved improvements will reflect not only on them personally, but also the entire organization as a whole.

- Provide ongoing follow-up budget sessions to address implications, issues and concerns.
- Get departmental managers directly involved in developing their own budgets and allowing them to voice their judgments and concerns, advance their ideas, and ask for allowances they believe are truly needed.
- Address the budgeting process from a, "What's in it for me?" perspective, such as how a budget helps to enable more objective evaluations of department heads that are under upper management's direction. It helps to find the positives of what is transpiring rather than dwelling only on various negative aspects.

## Deciding If a Fixed or "Static" Budgeting Approach Is Appropriate

A fixed budget is prepared based only on one level of output. It tends to remain unchanged irrespective of the level of activity actually attained and is therefore static in nature rather than dynamic. Within a fixed budget, the figures are for a *single* level of activity. Therefore, if the level of output actually achieved tends to differ considerably from that which is budgeted, large variances will arise.

Some companies, due to the nature of their business, are not suited to fixed budget preparation. These include ones that are:

- Directly affected by weather conditions or seasonal patterns
- Companies that frequently introduce new product lines such as a food canning industry
- Centered on production that is only carried out when orders are received from customers
- Affected by direct changes in specific trades or industries
- Export oriented

Under fixed budgets, managers are held responsible for variances that are not always under their control, including both fixed and variable costs. A fixed budget is never able to assess properly the true efficiency and actual performance of the manager. For example, take a fixed budget that is set with a planned 10,000 hours, but an actual 12,000 hours are recorded. From both the motivational or control point, it is difficult to gauge the actual efficiency of the manager(s) who are involved in the manufacture of the output at that actual level.

## Deciding If Dynamic Budgeting Is More Appropriate Than Static Budgeting

The more volatile the industry, the more there is a need for flexible budgeting. For all purposes, a flexible budget can be thought of as a "statement of projected revenue and expenditure that is based on various levels of production." It shows how costs vary with different rates of output or at different levels of sales volume. A flexible budget is an extremely useful tool for comparing the actual cost incurred to the cost allowable for the activity level achieved as it is dynamic in nature rather than static. A flexible budget is a budget that is designed to change in accordance with the *level of activity* attained. This type of budget recognizes the difference in cost behavior in relation to fluctuations in output or turnover.

In addition, a flexible budget:

- Is prepared for *different* levels of activity
- Is designed to change appropriately with fluctuation
- Allows more meaningful comparison as it "flexes" to actual volume
- Computes what costs should have been for the actual level of activity

A major benefit of deciding to take a flexible budget approach is that budgeting has the advantage of assisting managers to more effectively deal with uncertainty, by allowing them to see the expected outcomes for a range of activity.

## Flexible Budgeting Steps for Cost Control and Profit Planning

The sequential steps involved in preparing a flexible budget includes:

1. Selecting the measure of activity, such as the units of production;
2. Defining the relevant range of activity for the budgeted performance (which is based on step 1);

3. Identifying the cost items to be included within the budget;
4. Determining the cost behavior of each item over the relevant range;
5. Separating the cost items into "variable," "fixed" and "mixed";
6. Selecting the specific levels of activity to be budgeted;
7. Using the cost behavior (under item 4) to estimate the budgeted amounts for each cost item at the different levels selected, which are found in step 6.

## POINTS TO PONDER — SOMETHING TO THINK ABOUT

1. What type of budget have you normally operated under?
2. What types of problems have you encountered because of the form of budget you are working with?

## TRAINING ACTIVITY — APPLICATION & ACTION PLAN

A key to monitoring and maintaining a budget needs to include benchmarking activities and output. Focusing on a budget's bottom line without fully understanding why variances occur can lead to dysfunctional decision making.

In regard to management control, determine if some managers, supervisors or foremen use benchmarking to help eliminate overhead volume variances, then:

1. Discuss how benchmarking affects direct expensing of overhead to eliminate the potential for volume variances.
2. Discuss how benchmarking works to help identify the impacts of fixed overhead on per unit prices.

3. Discuss how benchmarking can be used to monitor the recovery of overhead expenses, as well as to help determine if and when fixed expenses should be reduced.
4. Discuss how effective performance evaluation requires differentiation of costs controllable by managers from those heavily influenced by external events. As part of the process, detail specific reasons as to why most administrators and managers are not able to control certain production outputs that have been set.
5. Discuss how monitoring various changes between actual and planned (standard) volume can help managers make necessary changes in budgeted fixed costs.
6. Discuss how effective management control requires an understanding as to how volume changes help achieve planned levels of performance and profits.
7. Discuss why it is important for departmental managers to determine whether variance was controllable and by whom.

# 7

# How Effective Analysis Impacts Decision Making

When asked the question, "Just what is a budget?" most every department head, manager, supervisor or foreman within an organization will likely respond, "A budget is a plan." Budgets are only superficially about numbers. At their core they are an expression of values. In other words, budgets tend to express what people and organizations care most about. Within the budgeting process it is important to address the resource challenges that constrain the ability to achieve the excellence to which an organization aspires to attain.

## IMPLICATIONS — WHAT THIS MEANS TO YOU

Budgets are an element of an organization's financial management. Financial management specifically addresses the overall fiscal integrity of an organization, which is an ongoing process. Although some aspects of financial management are cyclical, such as budget development, cost monitoring, forecasting, etc., financial management occurs on a daily basis.

The mission of the organization is to maximize the value of its output while minimizing associated costs, which is the common goal of all functions of an organization. As a common organizational element, departmental budgets emerge from the goals and objectives of the organization.

From an effective budgetary viewpoint, a budget becomes a plan of action that is matched by resources that are required to implement the plan. Budgets generally divide between two broad categories: the operating budget, sometimes known as the "expense" budget and the "capital" budget. When exploring and examining the two broad categories of "expense" and "capital" within various types of budgets, increasingly detailed information begins to unfold, which helps to clearly identify labor costs, materials costs and the overhead costs that are all associated with the budget/plan.

## STRATEGIES, TIPS & TECHNIQUES TO APPLY

### The Intentions of Effective Budgeting

Typically, all budgets are intended to serve three major purposes: planning, coordinating and controlling. These three functions dictate that budgeting and financial management remain flexible yet accountable throughout the fiscal period.

Budget planning affects organizational personnel from both bottom-up and top-down directions. From the top, senior management communicates organizational goals and objectives and expects that all lower-level functions within the organization align their objectives accordingly. From the bottom-up, all department head personnel, including managers, supervisors or foremen would theoretically be involved in the budget development process, especially that of line-item budget development. Regardless of the type of budget developed, the process represents an ideal time for all departmental personnel to be informed and involved in the financial planning process, since each department tends to complement one another within the entire organization.

Although many types of budgets exist, most organizations employ one of the following types: lump sum, formula, line-item, program, performance/function, or zero-based. Some will be more effective than others when serving a particular purpose.

### The Lump Sum Budget

Typically, lump sum budgets involve the allocation of funds by organizational upper-level management, which comes down as a "lump sum" of budget resources to individual departments. Since the lump sum method tends to lack specific ties to corporate goals and objectives, many department heads or managers prefer other types of budgets. However, lump sum budgets can be perceived as representing a high level of flexibility and control within the organization itself. Once the lump sum is allocated, each department head manager proceeds with lower-level allocations among various programs and activities.

## The Formula Budget

When a department is funded through a formula budget, the budget allocation is typically tied to a numeric value, such as full-time equivalencies, or (FTEs). These constitute the number of employees, which is multiplied by a fixed dollar amount that yields the budget for the department.

This budgeting technique harbors numerous weaknesses. One weakness stems from the fact that the budget total is calculated at a late point in time and intrudes on advance planning, especially for purchases and staffing increases within individual departments. Another weakness results from the formula budget's lack of identification with specific organizational goals and objectives. A third weakness comes from the unpredictable nature of the budget itself, since the formula is normally based on variables outside the influence or control of the department.

## The Line-Item Budget

The line-item budget represents the most commonly used budgeting method. Within it, each category of activity is afforded its separate appearance. Line-item budgets facilitate low levels of detail for both planning and cost control purposes. Often, the accounting function of the organization develops accounts and sub-accounts on a companywide basis. In that case, individual departments are required to use the company accounting scheme.

Line-item budgets demonstrate numerous advantages in their:

- Ease of preparation
- Ability to be used as a detailed planning vehicle

- Ability to serve as the major means for comparing performance from one fiscal period to another

Below is a simple model to illustrate the uncomplicated and straightforward nature of the line-item budget:

| | Last Year | This Year | Next Year |
|---|---|---|---|
| Salaries | | | |
| Materials | | | |
| Necessary Purchase | | | |
| Etc. | | | |
| Etc. | | | |
| Miscellaneous | | | |

Problems with line-item budgets often include the difficulty of relating the line budget to organizational goals. Since the line-item budget has a propensity for "perpetuating" a line, or in other words, "once a line … always a line," budgets can become highly ineffective. Also there is the tendency of the "Miscellaneous" line to grow unmanageably as technologies and other services or business-related necessities evolve with their associated costs. Finally, there is the reality that comparing "This year to Last year" becomes more complex, where the budget is required yet unable to represent unexpected variables, which then remain unaccounted for.

## The Program Budget

By its nature, a program budget focuses on the services or functions specific departments provide. On the positive side, the program budget technique more readily relates to overall organizational goals and objectives. Its attractiveness is further enhanced by its usefulness when establishing priorities for programs or initiatives that are more relative to the organization's strategic plan.

Program budget development is typically an extension of the line-item budget development method, but instead it details expenditures per individual program, which is designated by a given percentage of time that needs to be allocated for it. As part of its effectiveness, a program budget facilitates comparative analyses among multiple programs. It also has the ability to produce a document that is easily understood, and one that demonstrates a willingness to make best use of limited resources by minimizing conflict and overlap among projects.

One disadvantage associated with a program budget emerges when the adoption of the program budget method forces department heads to think along program lines, in contrast to the comfort zone associated with previous budgeting methods. It becomes easy for some department heads, managers, supervisors or foremen to become highly defensive when they are required to analyze, report and justify how their time is being spent.

A program budget typically resembles:

| | **Program 1** | **Program 2** | **Program 3** | **Total** |
|---|---|---|---|---|
| **Salaries** | | | | |
| **Materials** | | | | |
| **Necessary Purchases** | | | | |
| **Miscellaneous** | | | | |
| **Totals** | | | | |
| % | | | | 100% |

## The Performance Budget

Performance budgets tend to share similar characteristics with program budgets. However, performance budgets primarily focus on what departmental members do, or what functions they perform. Within this budgeting technique, tasks rather than programs are highlighted.

Among the functions displayed within a performance budget are technical services such as cataloging, materials processing, and planning functions, as well as budgeting, automation, employee selection, interviewing, development, and client or customer contact through email and telephone. Within this technique each function is broken down to detail a specific allotted amount.

An example of a performance budget:

| | Function 1 | Function 2 | Function 3 | Total |
|---|---|---|---|---|
| Salaries | | | | |
| Materials | | | | |
| Necessary Purchases | | | | |
| Miscellaneous | | | | |
| Totals | | | | |
| % | | | | 100% |

Performance budgets do have a specific strength. They can be used as an instrument for monitoring staff members and for developing unit costs. However, the primary disadvantage associated with the performance budget is there is more of an emphasis on quantity rather than on the quality of the activity being monitored.

## Zero-Based Budget

Zero-based budgets shift the emphasis from comparing past performance and/or programs to the present, or current, activity. Zero-based budgeting requires a "clean slate" starting point for budget development. Because of this, the emphasis is on "what will happen in the future" in a manner that directly corresponds to the organization's goals and objectives.

This "from scratch" approach is often viewed as an appropriate instrument to rank departmental programs by cost/importance to organizational goals, and to identify and eliminate certain programs that provide minimal value. Once value-enhancing activities become identified, their associated costs are subsequently developed.

The advantages associated with zero-based budgeting include its focus on identifying programs that will further the company's goals for the future. Reliance on "the way we've always done things" violates the basic premise of zero-based budgeting. Most zero-based budgeting advocates believe that the method promotes innovation, effectiveness and efficiency.

The downside of zero-based budgeting relates to its time-consuming nature. Beginning at "zero" implies that all aspects of a department's operation will undergo examination and justification. Numerous department heads who are forced to operate under zero-based budgeting tend to feel that it intrudes on many day-to-day operational activities.

## POINTS TO PONDER — SOMETHING TO THINK ABOUT

1. What type of budget do you feel would be best to employ in your organization? Why?
2. Can you think of several positive reasons for utilizing your current budgeting process in the future?

## TRAINING ACTIVITY — APPLICATION & ACTION PLAN

### Effective Project Measurement

Project measurements include strategies, tactics, and tools for managing and monitoring the implementation of project activity and its ongoing progress.

- It includes controlling key factors to ensure that the project's end result(s) matches scope and quality expectations, which are delivered on time and within budget.
- Successful project measurement requires an implementation of systems that will enable project delivery teams to control changes in the key factors of scope, costs, schedule, and quality.

Scheduling workload activity is necessary to ensure the success of any project. This includes developing a time-phased budget baseline to accompany it. Begin the process by:

## Scheduling Authorized Work

For each separate project, develop a schedule that works to integrate all of the technical, cost, and schedule aspects of the related work, which as an end result details the expected sequence of it.

Look for Interdependencies that can be established, which will result in generating the total amount of work time while simultaneously revealing the critical path, (which is also the shortest duration of the project).

Within each task identify objective interim measures that will allow for accurate monthly performance assessment.

A sufficient number of these interim measures will be defined after the detailed schedule is established to ensure the performance is measured as accurately as possible.

## Developing a Time-Phased Budget Baseline

A budget baseline must also be established and maintained. The assignment of budgets to work-related activities or tasks results in a plan against which actual performance can be measured.

This is referred to as the performance measurement baseline or (PMB), which should be established as early as possible after notice to proceed has been issued.

The PMB includes direct hours/dollars, direct material dollars, equipment and any other direct costs, and any indirect costs for the agreed scope.

The indirect costs associated with design, oversight, and management must also be included.

Essentially the PMB represents the formal plan for the project manager to accomplish all the work required in the time allotted and within the budget provided.

# 8

# Results and Outcomes

The budget process represents a means of obtaining buy-in from departmental personnel regarding the planned activities for the coming fiscal period. A budget serves as a pivot point for coordinating projects and programs among departmental personnel. Budgets represent a vehicle for sharing information regarding program mission, development, and implementation. When staff members have a global understanding of the available resources and the commitments of those resources, then those who are responsible for individual programs will function with a more perceptive knowledge of the department's and/or organization's finite resources.

## IMPLICATIONS — WHAT THIS MEANS TO YOU

Results and outcomes are obtained through effective budgetary monitoring and controlling, two terms that are often used interchangeably. When considering these two terms, the concept of performance standards represents a natural corollary. Along that same vein, budgets as an end product are the basic performance standards by which departments are measured. As such, results and outcomes of effective budgeting and financial analysis leads to more careful monitoring and measuring of project progress, as well as its related activity.

From an effective budgetary standpoint, within all levels of management, budgets typically represent an effective element of control, whether on a day-to-day operational or a longer-term basis. When budgets parallel organizational goals, then performing to budget standards can be realistically interpreted as "a reasonable element of control."

## STRATEGIES, TIPS & TECHNIQUES TO APPLY

### Earned Value Analysis: Measuring a Project's Progress

Applying the earned value analysis approach provides a basis for course correction and answers two essential questions:

1. At the end of the project, is it likely that the cost will be less than, equal to or greater than the initial estimate?
2. Will the project likely be completed on time as initially predicted?

Earned value analysis works most effectively when a project is broken down into an organized, incremental work structure. In other words, workloads become compartmentalized. The work break down structure is used as the basic building block for the complete planning process of a specific project. It is a product-oriented division of a project, which ensures that the entire scope of work is captured, which also allows for the integration of technical, schedule, and cost information.

### The Process of Earned Value Analysis

The methodology of earned value analysis works to break down the entire work scope into appropriate elements for planning, budgeting, scheduling, cost accounting, work authorization, progress measuring, and management control. The indirect costs of design, oversight, and management must be included so that they are reflected within the full budget.

### Calculating Earned Value

Earned value management measures progress against a baseline and involves calculating three key values for each activity:

1. **The Planned Value (PV)** (formerly known as the budgeted cost of work scheduled or BCWS) –That portion of the approved cost estimate planned to be spent on the given activity during a given period.

2. **The Actual Cost (AC)** (formerly known as the actual cost of work performed or ACWP) – The total of the costs incurred in accomplishing work on the activity in a given period. This actual cost must correspond to whatever was budgeted for the Planned Value and the Earned Value (i.e. all labor, material, equipment, and indirect costs).
3. **The Earned Value (EV)** (formerly known as the budget cost of work performed or BCWP) – Denotes the value of the work actually completed.

These three values need to be combined in order to determine at a given point in time whether or not work is being accomplished as planned. The most commonly used measures for this are the Cost and Schedule Variance, which are determined by the formulas:

**Cost Variance (CV) = EV – AC**

**Schedule Variance (SV) = EV – PV**

These two values can be converted to efficiency indicators in order to reflect the cost and schedule performance of the project.

The most commonly used cost-efficiency indicator is the Cost Performance Index, or (CPI). It is calculated as:

**CPI = EV / AC**

The sum of all individual EV budgets divided by the sum of all individual AC's is known as the Cumulative CPI, and is generally used to forecast the cost to complete a project.

The Schedule Performance Index or (SPI), is calculated as:

**SPI = EV / PV**

This is often used with the CPI to forecast overall estimates for project completion.

A negative Schedule Variance (SV), which is calculated at a given point in time, means the project is behind schedule, while a negative Cost Variance (CV) means the project is over budget.

## Budgeting for Other Positive Outcomes

The conventional approach to budgeting is fundamentally flawed, because it tends to focus entirely on what must be cut, while ignoring what should be kept. Many conventional budgeting approaches do little to improve the effectiveness of organizational initiatives. They also never work to enlarge upon or discuss the question of how to maximize the value of the dollars being spent.

To produce more effective budgeting outcomes it becomes important to get a handle on the main problem, which implies asking and answering: How much of the departmental budget is short-term, and how much is long-term? and, Are income or expenses or both driving the budget? As part of the process it becomes necessary to understand the set priorities of the organization. Once these are analyzed, it is important to identify and define the five or so outcomes that matter most, along with indicators to measure progress.

Once this is accomplished it becomes time to set the price or cost in relationship to each priority. To do this, divide the allocated (or necessary) revenue among the priority outcomes on the basis of their relative value to the organization.

## Develop a Budgeting Plan for Each Priority

In some departments it may be an effective move to create a "results team" to act as the budget process overseer. Once formulated, have the members in the team decide upon which projects, activities and strategies they believe will have the most impact on each organizational priority's desired outcome.

Have the team begin by developing a strategy map, using available evidence about what really matters. Next have the team generate a detailed cause and effect diagram, showing the best ways to achieve each desired outcome. With a cause and effect methodology, the team will be able to draw up a general budgeting plan, laying out the key strategies needed to produce each individual outcome.

## A Solid Budget Results in Focusing on the Need to Obtain Better Results

Generating higher levels of results means delivering higher-value departmental outcomes with the revenue that is available. The question is, "How to accomplish it?" The answer is often seen in smarter sizing, spending, management, and work processes. Below are several methods for helping to accomplish this:

## Strategic Reviews

Because time is short during budget season, smart department heads will create an ongoing review process, outside the budget process in order to develop new strategies and eliminate programs that are not central to their core purposes or are no longer highly valuable to the organization. There are many tools that can be used to comb through the organization from top to bottom, including program reviews, departmental interviews and internal surveys.

## Rightsizing

Some organizations work better when reduced in size, but others are crippled. Finding the right size does not start with layoffs. Rather, it starts by asking whether organizations are doing the right work, aimed at producing the right results, in the most effective way. Then, it is essential to make sure the organization has the right staff with the right mix of skills to maximize the value delivered. Eliminating bureaucratic layers and closing regional offices can often help an organization find the right size, while human-capital planning can help it develop the right skills.

## Rewarding Performance, Not Good Intentions

If departmental managers don't know exactly what they are getting for the money being spent from out of the budget, chances are they aren't getting much. The solution is to set performance targets at all levels, measure performance against them, and reward those who improve. The whole idea is to improve outcomes for less money: value for dollars.

## Don't Instill Mistrust—Eliminate It

The sad truth of organizational bureaucracy, is that much spending is designed merely to control employees and what they do and accomplish. The ruling assumption is that most people, if given the opportunity, will lie, cheat, and deceive and will do as little as possible when they can get by with it. Not only does this thinking undermine performance, it is incredibly expensive. The smarter move is to first win voluntary compliance by simplifying the rules, and educating employees, which makes the process of compliance easier without lowering performance standards, and to create incentives that reward compliance, while reserving punishment for those who willfully violate the rules.

## Using Flexibility to Get Accountability

Examples abound of performance-based organizations that have willingly accepted greater accountability in return for freedom from rules and regulations that impede performance. One way is to look upon departments as "freedom communities" in which they can be offered more flexibility if they improve their cost structures, services, and if they are able to create mechanisms to measure performance, verify it and report it to the organization.

## Making Administrative Systems Partners, Not Enemies

All organizations are creatures (or hostages) of their internal systems. Traditional budget, accounting, personnel, procurement, and audit systems often are nests of red tape that tie employees up in knots. The messages these systems send about following bureaucratic rules are much more powerful than any leadership initiative for performance enhancement. To gain lasting performance improvements, organizational management should seriously look at modernizing and streamlining these systems if they are not functioning as well as they could or should. The payoff is dramatic in terms of cost savings.

## POINTS TO PONDER — SOMETHING TO THINK ABOUT

1. Once budgets are in place do you feel it may be worthwhile to initiate employee performance agreements to help maintain performance standards and to help control project outcomes? Why or why not?
2. "Budgeting for Outcomes" focuses squarely on the need to "obtain better results." Within your department what do you feel this phrase implies?

## TRAINING ACTIVITY — APPLICATION & ACTION PLAN

Help create smarter work processes.

1. Within your department look at various productivity tools that can be applied to shorten work cycles or to support work projects and work-related activities.
2. To do more with less, organizational departments may have to change or modify the way they work, or at least portions of it.
3. This may involve the substitution of new methods and strategies, but much of it requires that existing work processes of all kinds—from station set-up to workflow alterations be modified.
4. Create a list of possible ways to shortcut one particular activity or some of its support work.
5. Detail the steps needed in order to modify or change how something will be done to accomplish the improvement in productivity.

# About the Author

Timothy F. Bednarz, Ph.D. is CEO of the American Management Development Group, Inc. For over 20 years he has researched, designed and authored hundreds of learning and development programs used by Fortune 1000 companies.

He is also the author of *Great! What Makes Leaders Great. What They Did, How They Did It and What You Can Learn from It* (2011).

## Speaking Availability

Timothy F. Bednarz, Ph.D. is available for speaking engagements for your next meeting or association event. He can be contacted at 800-654-4935 or by e-mail at timothy.bednarz@majorium.com.

## Bulk Sales

Bulk sales of this book or any other titles available from Majorium Business Press. Inquiries can be directed to sales@majorium.com, or by phone at 800-6654-4935.

# Quick Order Form

**Fax orders:** 715-342-1118. Send this form.

**Telephone orders:** Call 800-654-4935 toll-free. Have your credit card ready.

**Email orders:** sales@majorium.com

**Postal orders:** Majorium Business Press, 2025 Main Street, Stevens Point, WI 54481, USA.

**Please send the following books:**

________________________________________________________

________________________________________________________

________________________________________________________

________________________________________________________

**Please send more FREE information on:**

❑Catalog ❑Speaking/Seminars ❑Mailing Lists ❑Consulting

Name: ________________________________________________

Address: ______________________________________________

City: __________________________ State: _____ Zip: __________

Telephone: ____________________________________________

Email address: _________________________________________

**Sales tax:** Please add 5.5% for products shipped to Wisconsin addresses.

**Shipping by air:**

**United States:** $4.00 for first book and $2.00 for each additional product.

**International:** $9.00 for first book; $5.00 for each additional product (estimate).

Made in the USA
Monee, IL
07 November 2026

68002972R00039